4
Ingredients
Allergies

Kim
McCosker

4 Ingredients

Allergies

4 Ingredients
PO Box 400
Caloundra QLD 4551
Ph: (+61) 7 5341 8282

ABN: 17 435 679 521

FB: facebook.com/4ingredientspage
YT: 4 Ingredients Channel
W: 4ingredients.com.au
TW: @4ingredients

4 Ingredients Allergies

Photography:	Angie Simms, www.simmsquinn.com
	Glen Turnbull, www.4ingredients.com.au
Cover & Formatting:	Splitting Image
	www.splittingimage.com.au
Printing & Binding:	Leo Paper Group
Australia Publisher:	Simon & Schuster
New Zealand Publisher:	Random House
UK Publisher:	Simon & Schuster
USA Publisher:	Atria Books (a division of Simon & Schuster, USA)
ISBN:	978-0-9806294-4-6

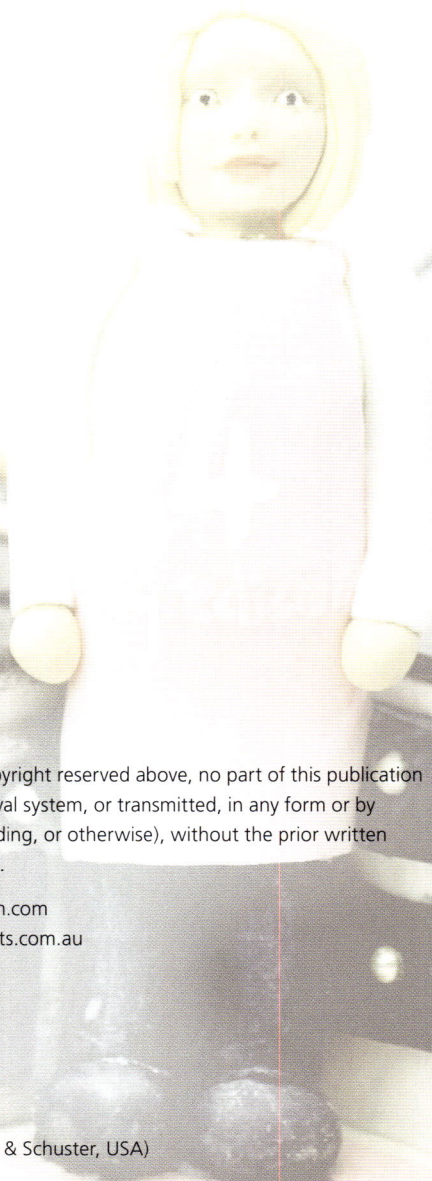

4 Ingredients Wellness Trilogy

I enjoy people. I love to engage with, talk with and listen to people. By nature I ask many questions, as my greatest learnings come from everyday, busy people – just like me. And it's often where the best ideas for future books and projects stem from – people just like you.

This is exactly how the *Wellness Trilogy* came to be. From conversations on our Facebook page, emails to info@4ingredients.com.au and your interest at my public engagements, the most frequently asked questions are; when are you bringing out a *4 Ingredients* book relating to Gluten, Lactose, Diabetes and Allergies? So for you all … *Here they are!*

Three beautiful, affordable books each with over 60 quick, easy and delicious recipes aimed to encourage us all; not only to eat better, but to prevent … *Prevention is the best Medicine!*

Watch for *Wellness Tips* **WT** throughout the trilogy.

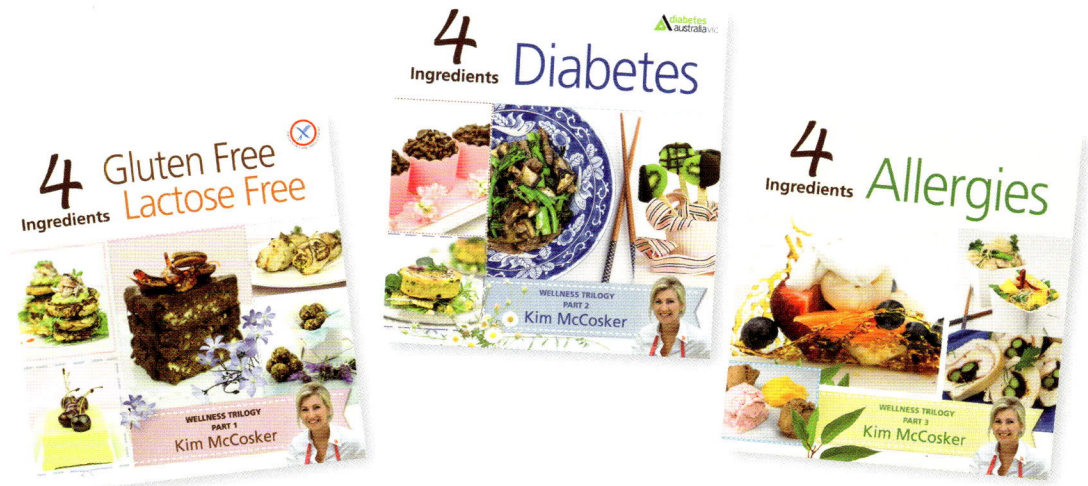

What is a Food Allergy?

A food allergy is an overreaction of the body's immune system to a specific part of a food, usually a protein. When someone is allergic to a food, the food they are allergic to is called the allergen. An allergy can be mild, a little more than uncomfortable or severe. People with an allergy have an immune system response to a substance which for most, is harmless. Triggers of allergic reactions include foods, medications, pollen, dustmite, latex, insect stings or bites and for a small minority, even exercise!

Food allergy and food intolerance are different although some of the signs and symptoms of reactions can be similar. Food intolerance is not an immune system response. Unlike food allergy, people with an intolerance to a food usually develop signs and symptoms many hours later and they generally involve the skin (hives, redness, swelling) and/or the gut. It is important that a person thought to have a food allergy or food intolerance consults their doctor for accurate diagnosis and management.

The Australasian Society of Clinical Immunology and Allergy (ASCIA – www.allergy.org.au) reports that about one in 20 children and one in 100 adults have food allergies. About 60 percent of allergies appear during the first year of life (cow's milk allergy is one of the most common in early childhood) but many children outgrow allergies to milk, egg, wheat and soy during their childhood years. ***The tendency to be allergic can be familial. Whilst you do not inherit food allergy***, children who have one family member with an allergic disease (such as asthma or eczema) have a 20 to 40 percent higher risk of developing an allergy of some sort. If there are two or more family members with allergic disease, the risk increases to 50 to 80 percent. This means that a child whose parents both have an allergic disorder such as eczema or asthma, is much more likely to develop eczema or allergic rhinitis (hay fever) or food allergy or asthma, or a combination of these conditions.

Allergy & Anaphylaxis Australia report that the most common triggers of food allergies are cow's milk, egg, peanuts, tree nuts (such as almond and cashew), wheat, sesame, soy, fish and shellfish (such as prawn, crab, lobster). Whilst these 9 foods are the cause of 90 percent of food allergic reactions in Australia and New Zealand any food can trigger an allergic reaction including anaphylaxis (most severe form of allergic reaction).

What Does Allergy-Free Mean?

4 Ingredients Allergies is a collection of recipes free of these 9 common allergens and was written to satisfy an ever-increasing market demand for allergy-free recipes.

Allergy-free: For the purpose of this cookbook allergy-free refers to a recipe or ingredient free of these 9 major allergens:

Cow's Milk	**Tree Nuts**	**Sesame**
Eggs	**Fish**	**Soy**
Peanuts	**Shellfish**	**Wheat**

Allergies have emerged as a major public health problem in developed countries during the twentieth century. *Australia and New Zealand have among the highest prevalence of allergic disorders in the developed world.* Children with allergies are present in almost every school classroom and in 2011 a large Victorian research study revealed that 1 in 10 babies born in Australia will develop a food allergy *(www.allergyfacts.org.au/about-us/foodallergyawareness)*.

4 Ingredients Allergies was written with guidance from:

Allergy & Anaphylaxis Australia

Allergy & Anaphylaxis Australia (A&AA) is a not for profit organisation that works tirelessly to inform, support, educate and advocate for the needs of individuals and families living with food allergy and to support and participate in research. A&AA also works closely with health professionals, food industry and other key stake holders in improving allergy management world-wide. For more detailed information please contact www.allergyfacts.org.au.

Allergy & Anaphylaxis
Australia
Your trusted charity for allergy support

Allergy New Zealand

Allergy New Zealand is a national membership-based, not-for-profit society. Their primary role is to provide information, education, and support to the many thousands of New Zealanders living with allergies, including those at risk of anaphylaxis, and to help them manage their or their child's allergy and live an active and healthy lifestyle.

Allergy New Zealand also represent their interests particularly to government, policy makers and the media, provide information and guidance to the health, education and food sectors, and support research. For more information contact www.allergy.org.nz.

WARNING

Every effort has been made to ensure the recipes in this cookbook list ingredients which are free of the 9 most common allergens listed above. However manufacturing processes can change as can ingredient labels. Always check the ingredients in any food you prepare, every time to prepare it.

Always check the labels on ingredients before buying or using, and avoid ingredients where there is a risk of cross-contamination e.g. bulk bins in supermarkets. If you have any concerns always check with the manufacturer. For allergen management information, specific to you or your child, speak with your family doctor or an accredited dietitian.

Anaphylaxis

The term comes from the Greek words
ἀνά **ana,** *against*, and φύλαξις **phylaxis**, *protection*.

Anaphylaxis

Anaphylaxis or anaphylactic shock is an extreme allergic reaction that is rapid in onset and is potentially life threatening. A severe allergic reaction/anaphylaxis involves the respiratory system and/or the cardiovascular system. Simply speaking this means difficulty breathing and/or deterioration in someone's level of consciousness/collapse because of low blood pressure. People having a severe reaction often also have skin symptoms such as hives and swelling and/or gut symptoms such as abdominal pain or vomiting but not always. The most common triggers of anaphylaxis include insect bites and stings, foods and medications. Anaphylaxis is uncommon but not rare, with new cases arising at rates of between 8.4 and 21 per 100 000. The prevalence of food allergy and anaphylaxis has increased significantly in the last 10 year period *(Mullins R J. Anaphylaxis: risk factors for recurrence.* Clin Exp Allergy *2003; 33: 1033-1040).*

Food

Many foods can trigger anaphylaxis; this may occur upon the first known ingestion. In Western cultures world-wide, peanuts, tree nuts, shellfish, fish, wheat, milk, and eggs are the most common culprits. Sesame is more common in the Middle East and less common in the USA, while buckwheat is the most common trigger in Japan. Severe cases are almost always caused by eating the allergen (even a small amount) and some people experience a mild to moderate reactions upon skin contact.

Diagnosis

Food allergy must be diagnosed by an allergy specialist or a doctor with experience in food allergy. Diagnosis is based on the persons history (i.e., what happened when they ate the food) and skinprick/blood test results. A skin prick/blood test alone does not indicate someone may be at risk of anaphylaxis. Those at increased risk of anaphylaxis are prescribed an adrenaline autoinjector (EpiPen® or Anapen® in Australia and New Zealand). Adrenaline is first aid treatment for anyone having a severe allergic reaction.

The Good News

By age 16, 80 percent of children with a severe allergy to milk or eggs can tolerate these foods. Children with wheat or soy allergy also often outgrow their allergy. The majority of those with peanut, tree nut, fish, shellfish, and sesame allergy will have their allergy for life. The good news for these people is that with education, it is manageable. Although food allergy does impact on quality of life for the most part, with education and support, it is a manageable condition. In the words of Allergy & Anaphylaxis Australia, "Awareness, Avoidance, Action – Knowledge for life".

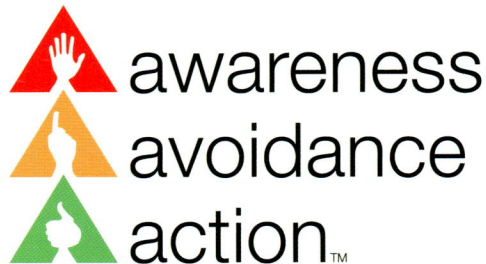

awareness
avoidance
action™

Knowledge for Life. ©2008 Allergy & Anaphylaxis Australia

Table of Contents

Breakfast

A healthy breakfast should contain fruits or vegetables, low-fat protein, dairy and whole grains. It is the combination of fibre, carbohydrates, protein and a small amount of fat that helps provide the nutrients required for good health and to keep you from getting hungry too quickly.

Apple & Date Quinoa Porridge

Serves 4

- *1 cup (170g) raw quinoa, rinsed*
- *1 small apple, thinly sliced*
- *⅓ cup dried dates (cranberries or raisins)*
- *½ teaspoon cinnamon*

In a saucepan, combine quinoa with 2 cups (500ml) water. Cover and bring to the boil. Reduce heat to low and simmer covered for about 5 minutes. Add apples, dates and cinnamon and simmer until all water is absorbed.

WT *Quinoa (pronounced: Keen-wah) is a nutritious ingredient with a nutty flavour that cooks like a grain and provides the same protein punch as meat, minus the fat and cholesterol – it's a fabulous addition to any breakfast!*

Breakfast Stack

Serves 2

- *4 slices allergy-free bacon, rind removed*
- *2 large field mushrooms, stalks removed*
- *8 cherry tomatoes*
- *6 asparagus spears, trimmed*

Heat a nonstick frying pan over medium heat and cook the bacon until crispy or cooked to your liking. Set aside on absorbent paper. In the same pan, brown the mushrooms and tomatoes for 2 minutes. Turn and cook for 2 minutes more. Add the asparagus and season with sea salt and cracked pepper. Transfer the mushrooms to a serving plate. Layer with bacon, asparagus and tomatoes.

WT *Customise a good 'stack' anyway you like. Substitute any of the above with avocado slices, wilted baby spinach or slices of grilled tomato. Slices of sweet potato first boiled, then fried in a little olive oil with garlic is also really scrummy.*

Chunky Bacon & Potato Hash

Serves 2

- *4 slices allergy-free bacon, rind removed*
- *½ red onion, roughly diced*
- *200g potato, peeled and par boiled, cut into chunks*
- *1 small red capsicum, roughly diced*

Heat a nonstick frying pan over medium heat, and cook the bacon until nice and crisp. Set aside on absorbent paper. In the same pan add the onion and potatoes and fry until potatoes just turn golden. Add capsicum and cook for 4 to 5 minutes until tender. Return bacon to pan and toss through. Season to taste and serve hot.

WT *Serve sprinkled with freshly chopped parsley or rosemary. Herbs not only boost flavour in meals, but your health too!*

Coyo with Blueberry Couli

Coyo (a coconut milk yoghurt) is a creamy delicious alternative to dairy yoghurt made from the milk of the coconut with plant fed probiotic cultures and it's delicious.

Serves 2

- *300g frozen blueberries*
- *2 tablespoons (40ml) agave nectar*
- *1 teaspoon orange zest*
- *400g Coyo*

Place the first 3 ingredients in a saucepan with 2 tablespoons of water. Over a medium to high heat, cook for 8 minutes, stirring occasionally to break up the blueberries, until a yummy syrup results. Meanwhile, divide the Coyo across two glasses and serve drizzled with the warm blueberry couli.

WT *The coconut tree is often referred to as the "Tree of Life" because of the endless list of products and by-products derived from its various parts.*

Frappacino

Serves 2

- *1 cup (250ml) strongly-brewed coffee, chilled*
- *2 teaspoons raw cacao powder*
- *½ cup (125ml) coconut milk*
- *3 tablespoons (60g) raw honey*

Place all ingredients in a blender along with 2 cups of ice cubes and blend until you have an icy slushy.

WT *Juices, Smoothies and Frappes are increasing in popularity to recharge or kick start your batteries. They are simple, delicious and nutritious. Here is another,* **The Vitamin C Superstar***: 2 kiwi fruit, peeled + 1 whole orange, peeled and deseeded + 6 large strawberries hulled. Blend and serve over ice with a twist of mint.*

Herbed Hash Browns

Makes 12

- *4 potatoes, peeled*
- *2 cloves crushed garlic*
- *2 sprigs rosemary, picked and finely chopped*
- *3 tablespoons (60g) olive oil*

Coarsely grate potatoes, then using hands, squeeze out as much excess liquid as possible and put into a bowl. Add garlic and rosemary and season well with sea salt and cracked pepper. In a large nonstick frying pan, add one tablespoon of oil and heat until shimmering but not smoking. Place 4 x quarter-cup portions of potato mixture in the pan and gently flatten each using a spatula. Cook over medium heat for 2 minutes or until browned. Turn and cook the other side until crisp and golden brown. Remove hash brown and drain on absorbent paper. Repeat with remaining mixture. These are also delicious served as a side with a meal.

WT *If you have some Coyo leftover from page 18 then simply mix a little with a splash of lemon juice, crushed garlic, fresh mint and chilli, season with sea salt and cracked pepper and dollop atop freshly made Hash Browns … YUM YUM YUM!*

Mango & Lychee Fruit Salad

Serves 2 to 4

- *2 mangoes*
- *24 lychees, peeled and deseeded*
- *1 lime*
- *6 fresh mint leaves*

Slice the cheeks from the mangoes and dice the flesh. Pop into a serving bowl and add lychees. Drizzle with the juice of half a lime and gently toss. Cover and chill in the fridge for at least 20 minutes, allowing time for the flavours to mingle. Just before serving, shred mint and stir into the salad. Garnish with a few mint sprigs and serve.

WT *Serve this sprinkled with your favourite hi-fibre (at least 5 or more grams of fibre per serving) wholegrain, allergy-free muesli and a dollop of Coyo or allergy-free yoghurt.*

Quinoa & Blueberry Smoothie

Makes 1

- *1 cup (170g) cooked quinoa*
- *1 banana, frozen*
- *1 cup frozen blueberries*
- *½ cup (125g) Coyo*

Place all the ingredients in a blender, and mix until smooth. The quinoa lends a subtle nutty flavour to your smoothie that perfectly balances the sweetness of the fruit … So yummy and super healthy!

WT *Packed with protein, calcium and fibre; quinoa is delicious, nutritious DYNAMITE! It is such an adaptable ingredient; it is a seed but cooks like rice, making it the perfect substitute for almost any grain. I use it in my kitchen as a breakfast, in my salads with a little olive oil, lemon juice and fresh herbs and as a base for deliciously moist cakes.*

Raw Tapioca Breakfast Puddings

Prepare this the night before so it's ready first thing in the morning.

Serves 2

- *1 cup (250ml) coconut milk*
- *2 tablespoons chia seeds*
- *1 tablespoon (20g) pure maple syrup (agave or rice malt)*

Pour the coconut milk into a bowl, add the chia seeds and pure maple syrup. Stir well, cover and refrigerate for at least 1 hour. The seeds will plump up, absorbing the liquid, leaving a delicious 'tapioca-like' pudding.

WT *Honestly, you are going to love this when you make it. It is unbelievably easy and incredibly tasty. Serve it with freshly chopped seasonal fruits and sprinkled with pumpkin seeds. Always check with your physician first, but often (not always) people with nut allergies can safely eat seeds; sunflower, pumpkin and flax in particular.*

Lunch

Collectively, it is our duty to educate everyone about the risks associated with food allergy and anaphylaxis, and put strategies in place to minimise exposure to known allergens.

KNOWLEDGE IS POWER

Chicken & Avocado Salad

Serves 4

- *1 cup (250ml) allergy-free caramelised balsamic vinegar*
- *4 chicken breasts, sliced*
- *4 Roma tomatoes, quartered*
- *3 avocados, sliced*

In a bowl mix half the balsamic with the chicken, marinate for 30 minutes. Heat a nonstick frying pan over medium / high heat and cook the chicken for 6 to 8 minutes turning regularly until golden and cooked. Remove from heat. When cooled, place in a mixing bowl, add tomatoes and avocados and gently toss. Drizzle with remaining balsamic. To serve season with sea salt and cracked pepper and a sprinkle of fresh basil leaves.

WT *To make your own delicious **Caramelised Balsamic Vinegar** see 4 Ingredients Gluten Free Lactose Free page 80: Simply; place ⅓ cup (80ml) balsamic vinegar, ⅔ cup (160ml) olive oil, 2 teaspoons caster sugar and 1 tablespoon chopped chives in a jar, seal and shake really, really well. Adjust seasonings if required!*

Cinnamon & Sage Sweet Potato Pasta

YUM YUM YUM!

Serves 4

- *2 long sweet potatoes*
- *2 tablespoons (40ml) olive oil*
- *1 tablespoon cinnamon*
- *2 tablespoons sage*

Wash and peel sweet potatoes, then using a vegetable peeler, peel lengthwise into thin strips. Heat the olive oil in a large nonstick frying pan over medium heat. Add the 'pasta', cinnamon and sage. Cook, stirring for 3 to 4 minutes or until just tender.

WT *Pasta makes for an easy and economical vegetarian meal especially when it is made from vegetables! Try making the **Tri-Coloured Pasta** from 4 Ingredients KIDS using 1 zucchini, 1 parsnip and 1 sweet potato. Use a vegetable peeler to peel thin strips from each, pop into a pot of salted boiling water for 2 to 3 minutes or until tender, drain and serve tossed with your family's favourite allergy-free pasta sauce!*

Noodle Boxes

Chicken Stir-fry

Serves 4

- 2 tablespoons (40ml) allergy-free balsamic vinegar
- 250g rice noodles
- 500g chicken breast stir-fry
- 250g broccolini

Combine vinegar and a quarter teaspoon of sea salt in a small bowl and mix well until the salt dissolves, taste the mixture (it should taste very similar to soy sauce). Add more salt if required. Prepare the noodles by soaking in a bowl of boiling water for 5 minutes or until tender. Drain and rinse. Heat a nonstick pan and when hot add chicken strips, sauté for 2 minutes. Add broccolini and stir-fry for 3 minutes. Add the noodles and balsamic mixture and toss through. Serve in noodle boxes with forks or chop sticks.

Mango, Chilli & Coriander

Serves 4

- 250g rice noodles
- 1 ripe mango, peeled and cut into strips
- 1 long fresh chilli, deseeded and thinly sliced
- 2 tablespoons freshly chopped coriander

Prepare the noodles as above. Add remaining ingredients, season with sea salt and cracked pepper and toss to combine. Serve.

Olive Chicken Koftas

Makes 8

- *1 cup (180g) cooked brown rice*
- *½ cup (160g) allergy-free olive tapenade*
- *500g lean chicken mince*
- *1 tablespoon (20ml) olive oil*

In a large bowl, mix the first three ingredients together. With wet hands, shape into 8 short, thick sausages. Add the oil to a nonstick frying pan over medium heat and cook for 3 minutes, turn and cook for a further 3 to 4 minutes or until cooked through. Serve drizzled with leftover Coyo dip (see Wellness Tip page 22) and this olive tapenade.

Olive Tapenade

Makes 1 cup

- *1 cup pitted kalamata olives*
- *1 clove garlic, crushed*
- *2 tablespoons finely chopped fresh basil*
- *1½ tablespoons (30ml) olive oil*

Place all the ingredients in a blender and process until smooth-ish. Spoon into a sealed jar and refrigerate for up to a week.

Potato Cakes

Serves 4

- *6 russet potatoes, peeled and cut into 1cm pieces*
- *1 leek (white and light-green parts only), halved lengthwise, rinsed well and thinly sliced*
- *100g English spinach*
- *4 slices allergy-free bacon, rind removed and chopped*

In a large pot of salted water, bring the potatoes to a boil. Reduce the heat to a rapid simmer, about 15 minutes. When the potatoes are just tender, add leek and spinach to blanch. Drain, transfer to a large bowl. In a large nonstick frying pan, cook the bacon over medium until crisp. Add to the bowl of veggies and season with sea salt and cracked pepper. Mash the mixture until just a few lumps remain. With clean, damp hands, form into 12 patties. Cook in the bacon juices in the frying pan over a medium/high heat for 3 minutes, flip and cook for another 3 minutes or until golden on both sides.

Stuffed Peppers

Makes 4

- *2 large red capsicums (peppers), cut in half lengthways*
- *500g lean beef mince*
- *1 medium onion, finely chopped*
- *2 celery stalks, finely chopped*

Preheat the oven to 180°C. Prepare the capsicums by scraping out membrane and seeds. In a nonstick frying pan, over medium heat cook the beef, onions and celery, seasoning well with sea salt and cracked pepper. Spoon the mixture into the capsicum halves and place on a baking tray. Bake for 30 minutes. Serve immediately.

WT *I love stuffed capsicums or peppers, they are a great way to use leftovers. The above is also nice with a sprinkle of cumin seeds and celery salt added when cooking mince. Another fresh tasting variation is a mix of cooked quinoa, Coyo, lemon zest, crushed garlic and fresh torn basil leaves. Mix together and spoon into capsicum cases. Bake for 30 minutes.*

Veggie Kebabs

Makes 8

- *1 red capsicum*
- *1 Spanish onion*
- *¼ fresh pineapple*
- *16 button mushrooms*

Cut the first three ingredients into chunks and thread alternately with mushrooms onto pre-soaked wooden skewers. Grill on a hot BBQ for 2 to 3 minutes each side, or until soft and tender.

WT *Serve with our delicious allergy-free* **Chilli & Honey Dressing**: *1 red birdseye chilli, seeds removed and finely chopped (to spread their deep, fiery heat) + 2 tablespoons raw honey + juice of 2 limes and 1 teaspoon freshly grated ginger … Whisk and ENJOY!*

Sides, Salads & Sauces

KNOW THE 9!

When it comes to food allergies, 90% of reactions
are caused by only 9 foods!

They are cow's milk, eggs, peanuts, tree nuts
(e.g. cashew, almond, walnut), fish, shellfish (e.g. prawn,
crab, lobster) soy, wheat and sesame.

Asparagus Fences

Serves 4

- *20 fresh asparagus spears*
- *1 tablespoon (20ml) olive oil*
- *1 garlic clove, crushed*
- *½ lemon, juice and zest*

Trim the woody ends of the asparagus. Thread 5 asparagus spears onto two skewers, crossways. Whisk oil, garlic, lemon juice and zest in a small bowl. Season well with sea salt and cracked pepper. Preheat BBQ grill or pan on medium. Brush a little of the oil mixture over the asparagus spears. Cook for 3 minutes each side, basting regularly with remaining oil until bright green and tender.

WT *To prepare green asparagus, simply snap off the whiter ends with your forefinger and thumb. Alternatively, run a knife along the stalk until it meets less resistance, then cut the end off at that point. Don't discard the woody part, there are many recipes, like soups and stews where, when cut properly and boiled, this part of the stalk will add flavour and texture to the dish.*

Creamy Avocado Mash

So good, so good, so good!

Serves 4

- *500g potatoes (Spunta, Sebago or Coliban are some of the varieties ideal for mashing)*
- *2 medium avocados*
- *1 tablespoon (20ml) lemon juice*

Peel and quarter the potatoes. Place the potatoes in a large pot with enough cold, salted water to cover them. Bring to the boil and simmer for 15 to 20 minutes or until tender. Drain, reserving a quarter cup of cooking water. Using a potato masher, roughly mash the potatoes. Add the avocado and lemon juice and beat with a wooden spoon until fluffy. Season with sea salt and cracked pepper. Gradually add the warm reserved water and beat to create a soft creamy texture. Season to taste. Delicious served with **Balsamic Glazed Chicken** (page 70), beef, lamb or pork.

WT *I just love the versatility of avocados. Make a delicious allergy-free ice cream mixing equal parts avocado and banana, freezing and blending. Toss a few slices of creamy avocado in salads or on burgers for a burst of buttery flavour. Or, my all-time favourite **Guacamole**; dice the flesh of 2 avocados, add 1 small diced tomato, ½ Spanish onion finely diced, and 2 tablespoons freshly chopped coriander, season and serve with fresh carrot and celery sticks.*

Dressings

Pineapple & Chilli

Makes 2 cups

- *2 cups fresh pineapple, cored and chopped*
- *1 chilli, deseeded and chopped*
- *2 tablespoons freshly chopped coriander*
- *1 lemon, juiced*

Place all ingredients in a blender and puree. Season with sea salt and cracked pepper. This is glorious served over grilled chicken.

WT *A pineapple is ripe if you gently tug on one of its leaves and it pulls easily from the fruit.*

Lychee & Mint

Makes 1 cup

- *12 fresh lychees, peeled and seeded*
- *8 mint leaves, chopped*
- *¼ cup (60ml) rice wine vinegar*
- *¼ cup (60ml) vegetable oil*

Combine the lychees, mint and vinegar in a blender and purée on low speed. Slowly add the oil until emulsified (may need to add a little extra). Season to taste and store in a tightly sealed jar in the refrigerator. This is delicious drizzled over salads or grilled chicken.

Mushroom & Thyme Kebabs

A delicious accompaniment with grilled chicken, beef and pork steaks, or as the 'Star of the Show' served with a fresh, healthy salad.

Serves 8

- *500g button mushrooms*
- *2 tablespoons (40ml) olive oil*
- *8 twigs fresh thyme, picked*
- *1 garlic clove, crushed*

Preheat grill for medium heat. Thread mushrooms onto metal skewers (otherwise soaked wooden skewers). In a small bowl, mix together olive oil, thyme and garlic and season with sea salt and cracked pepper. Brush the mushrooms with the oil and place kebabs on the grill. Baste frequently. Cook for 3 to 4 minutes, turning regularly, or until the mushrooms are tender and thoroughly cooked.

Napolitana Sauce

Makes 1 (400ml) jar

- *1 onion finely chopped*
- *3 cloves garlic, crushed*
- *4½ cups of diced Roma tomatoes*
- *¼ cup fresh basil leaves, coarsely torn*

Cook onion and garlic in a nonstick frying pan over medium heat. Add the tomatoes, season with sea salt and cracked pepper and bring to the boil. Reduce heat and allow to simmer uncovered until reduced by one-third, about 20 minutes. Stir in fresh basil.

WT *This is delicious served over grilled fish or chicken, sprinkled with capers and chopped olives. Slow cooked over meatballs, drizzled over roasted vegetables such as eggplant or zucchini or as a foundation ingredient for pizza and pasta … However you eat it, enjoy it!*

Pawpaw & Pineapple Salad

Serves 4

- *1 small pineapple, peeled*
- *1 red pawpaw, peeled*
- *1 red chilli, deseeded and chopped*
- *1 tablespoon (20ml) rice wine vinegar*

Use a sharp knife to remove the eye from the pineapple, then cut into paper thin slices. Cut the pawpaw into quarters, remove seeds and slice thinly. Arrange fruits on a flat serving plate. Combine chilli and vinegar and drizzle over. Serve chilled with a sprinkle of fresh mint if you have some.

Pawpaw, Mango & Green Tea Granita

- *2 cups (500ml) green tea*
- *1 small pawpaw*
- *1 mango*

Prepare tea as usual, and then cool. Pour into 3 ice cube trays and freeze. The next day, peel, deseed and dice the pawpaw and mango. Add green tea ice cubes to a blender and pulse until crushed. Add the fruits and process until smooth, making sure there are no large pieces remaining. Spoon into glasses or bowls and serve … *YUM!*

Salsas

Mango

Makes 2 cups

- *1 mango, peeled and diced*
- *1 avocado, diced*
- *1 vine ripened tomato, finely diced*
- *½ red onion, finely chopped*

Mix all ingredients together and season with sea salt and cracked pepper. Serve over grilled chicken, fish or pork.

Mint

Makes 2 cups

- *2 vine ripened tomatoes, finely diced*
- *1 small cucumber, diced*
- *2 tablespoons spring onion, sliced*
- *1 teaspoon fresh mint, chopped*

Mix tomatoes, cucumber and onion. Season before tossing mint through. Allow to stand for 10 minutes. Serve over grilled lamb or allergy-free sausages.

Plum Jam

Serves 4

- *2 cups chopped plums, skin removed*
- *1 cup (220g) sugar*
- *1 tablespoon (20ml) lemon juice*

Cook the plums and lemon juice on medium heat for 5 minutes. Add sugar and stir until everything is well combined. Cook for an additional 15 to 20 minutes until the thickness of the jam has been reduced to the consistency of honey. Skim off the foam and remove from heat. Pour into a warm jam jar and let cool completely before sealing. This will keep in the fridge for up to 3 weeks.

Plum Stir-fry Sauce

Serves 4

- *1 cup plum jam*
- *1 clove of garlic, crushed*
- *1cm fresh ginger, peeled and finely grated*
- *2 tablespoons (40ml) white vinegar*

Combine all ingredients and cook on the stovetop, stirring, over a low / medium heat until it starts to boil. Remove from heat and serve, or allow to cool and store in a sealed jar in the refrigerator. This is the sauce I used in the delicious **Plum & Ginger Pork Stir-fry,** page 80.

Quick Tomato Chutney

Makes 1 cup

- *3 large tomatoes, chopped*
- *½ small brown onion, finely diced*
- *2 tablespoons brown sugar*
- *1 tablespoon (20ml) red wine vinegar*

In a saucepan, place all ingredients together and cook over a low heat for around 8 to 10 minutes. Season and serve warm with grilled chicken or steak or homemade fries.

Pesto

Makes 1 cup

- *4 cups fresh basil or one bunch, rinsed and trimmed*
- *½ lemon, juiced*
- *1 clove garlic, peeled*
- *¼ cup (60ml) olive oil*

Place all ingredients in a blender or food processor and season really well with sea salt and cracked pepper. Blend until the mixture is completely pureed. Use more or less olive oil to adjust to desired consistency.

WT *Serve this pesto with grilled chicken, fish or as an accompaniment to roasted vegetables. If you have no cow's milk allergy or lactose intolerance, ¼ cup of grated Parmesan cheese is also lovely, as is a big healthy handful of spinach (you just may need a little extra oil). For a quick and easy* **Onion Marmalade** *see page 88.*

Mains

Food Labelling

If you have a food allergy, or shop for someone who does, it is essential to carefully read the ingredient label on any pre-packed food you buy.

Food labelling rules in Australia and New Zealand state that the 9 most common allergens — peanut, tree nuts, milk, egg, fish, shellfish, wheat, sesame and soy — must be declared on packaging. Some food, such as foods sold fresh in delicatessens, must either have ingredients displayed or have information about ingredients available in case a customer asks about allergen content.

Beware that other words may be used to refer to the allergen e.g., the words casein or whey may be used instead of the word milk.

Bacon & Wild Mushroom Risotto

Serves 4

- *200g allergy-free bacon, rind removed and chopped*
- *250g mushrooms, sliced*
- *1 litre allergy-free vegetable stock*
- *1 cup (185g) Arborio rice*

In a large nonstick frying pan over moderate heat, fry the bacon for 2 minutes. Add the mushrooms, season with cracked pepper and cook, uncovered, stirring occasionally, for 4 minutes or until the mushrooms soften. Meanwhile, place the stock in a saucepan and bring to a gentle boil, add the rice and stir well. Cook for 12 minutes or until firm to the bight. Add the bacon and mushrooms and stir. Cook for 6 minutes stirring occasionally, or until most of the stock has been absorbed and the rice is tender. Serve immediately.

WT *Rice is a pantry staple in my house. It is low in fat, salt and has no cholesterol. Risottos are a delicious, delicate alternative to pasta, they are much easier to prepare than people think and are extremely versatile. Try mixing allergy-free prosciutto and peas for the perfect combination of sweet and salty.*

Balsamic Glazed Chicken

Serves 4

- ¼ cup (80ml) allergy-free balsamic vinegar
- 2 tablespoons brown sugar
- 1 clove garlic, crushed
- 4 chicken thighs, sliced in half lengthways

Combine vinegar, sugar and garlic and pour over chicken thighs. Marinate for 1 hour. Grill or roast in a 170°C oven for 30 to 40 minutes or until cooked through and the flavourful sauce has caramelised.

WT *Serve this scrummy chicken with* **Grilled Zucchini Strips**: *Simply slice 2 zucchinis lengthways and heat a nonstick frying pan over moderate heat. In a little garlic infused olive oil grill the zucchini, drizzle with lemon juice and season with sea salt and cracked pepper.*

Caramelised Pineapple Pork

Serves 4

- *4 lean pork butterfly steaks*
- *1 small pineapple, peeled, cored and cut into 2cm thick wedges*
- *2 medium red chillies, finely sliced*
- *1 tablespoon brown sugar*

Half an hour prior to cooking, remove the pork from the fridge and bring to room temperature. This will help cook the steaks evenly. Season steaks generously with sea salt and cracked pepper. Heat a nonstick pan to medium / high and add pork. Cook for 5 to 7 minutes each side, turning just the once. Coat the pineapple wedges in brown sugar. Remove pork from pan to rest and add the sugared wedges and chilli to the pan juices. Cook, turning once and shaking often, until golden brown. Serve the caramelised pineapple with the pork steaks.

WT *Garnishing meals with fresh herbs not only adds a delicious texture and taste but much needed minerals and vitamins. I garnished this delicious dish with freshly picked coriander from my Dad's herb garden ~ Thanks Dadda!*

'Green' Lamb Cutlets with Chickpea Puree

Serves 4

- *12 lamb cutlets*
- *300g can chickpeas*
- *½ cup allergy-free Dijon mustard*
- *12 chives, finely chopped*

On a BBQ grill over high heat, cook the cutlets for 4 minutes each side or until done to your liking. Cover with foil and set aside to rest for 5 minutes. Drain the chickpeas, reserving half the liquid, then blend, adding reserved liquid to form a smooth puree, season well. 'Paint' the lamb cutlets with mustard and sprinkle with chives. Serve on a platter with a dollop of chickpea puree.

Mustard Glazed Roast Beef

Serves 4

- *2kg beef topside*
- *2 tablespoons (60g) raw honey*
- *2 tablespoons (40g) allergy-free wholegrain mustard*

Preheat oven to 220°C. Trim most of the fat from the piece of beef. Mix together the raw honey and mustard and brush over the roast in a thick layer. Place in a roasting tray and bake for 15 minutes, reduce the temperature to 180°C and continue to cook for 1 to 1½ hours for medium, or until done to your liking.

(WT) *I made this for my Dad's 65th birthday. To his delight, I served it with **Creamy Avocado Mash** page 50, steamed greens and with a side of homemade **Olive Tapenade** page 38.*

Paprika Crusted Pork with Bean 'Smash'

Serves 4

- *1 tablespoon paprika*
- *420g can cannellini beans, drained*
- *⅔ cup (300g) allergy-free salsa*
- *4 lean pork chops, or cutlets*

Combine paprika with cracked pepper and sea salt in a shallow container or clean plastic bag. Add pork cutlets and toss to coat evenly. In a nonstick frying pan cook the chops for 3 to 4 minutes each side or until cooked through. Remove from direct heat and rest for 3 minutes. Meanwhile, combine the beans and salsa and over a moderate heat, cook until warm. Using a masher, 'smash' the mixture together until you have a chunky but blended consistency. Serve the lovely bean smash over the spicy chops ... *YUM SCRUM!*

WT *Legumes are a staple food all over the world and are one of the best sources of soluble fibre. Plus, they're low in fat, high in protein and really economical. Beans are notoriously bland-tasting, but that's what makes them so versatile. They readily absorb flavours, add them to soups, stews, salads, casseroles, and dips.*
***NOTE:** Although peanut is also a legume, most people with peanut allergy can eat other legumes. If you are unsure, check with your doctor.*

Plum & Ginger Pork Stir-fry

Serves 4

- *500g lean pork, cut into chunks*
- *¾ cup (300g) plum stir-fry sauce (page 60)*
- *1 tablespoon freshly grated ginger*
- *200g snow peas*

Combine the pork pieces, sauce and ginger in a bowl, cover and marinate in the fridge for one hour. In a wok or frying pan, stir-fry the pork, in batches for 4 minutes, tossing to brown evenly, or until almost cooked. Return all of the pork to the pan, add the snow peas and stir-fry for 1 minute. To serve, season with cracked pepper, freshly shredded ginger and boiled rice.

WT *Ginger has many healthy benefits, and in this dish adds a lovely, fresh flavour. It also makes a beautiful herbal tea; simply steep a piece of peeled ginger in hot water with raw honey and a slice of lemon.*

Polenta Cake

Serves 6

- *1 litre allergy-free vegetable stock*
- *1 teaspoon mixed dried herbs*
- *1 cup (100g) raw polenta*

Preheat oven to 180°C. Line a 20cm cake tin with baking paper. In a saucepan over medium / high heat, bring the vegetable stock and herbs to a rolling boil. Reduce to a medium heat, add polenta gradually, stirring constantly to avoid clumps, until the mixture thickens. Pour the batter into the prepared tin and bake until golden, about 10 to 15 minutes. Serve warm. This is a great base for a variety of toppings. For the photo, I cut the cake into wedges and topped each with these yummy options:

WT **Onion Marmalade** *(page 88), Roasted Grapes & Thyme, Roasted Garlic, Mushrooms & Tomatoes and a raw Beetroot, Carrot & Apple Salad: In a blender, lightly pulse raw beetroot, carrot and apple, then dress with fresh lemon juice and chopped coriander. Pile each topping onto the polenta wedges and enjoy!*

Pumpkin & Cherry Tomato Risotto

Serves 4

- *300g pumpkin, peeled and chopped*
- *150g cherry tomatoes*
- *1 litre allergy-free vegetable stock*
- *1 cup (185g) Arborio rice*

Preheat the oven to 220°C. Lay the pumpkin in an even layer on a large paper lined baking tray. Season with sea salt and cracked pepper and roast for 10 to 15 minutes or until tender. Remove tray from oven, add tomatoes and roast for a further 6 minutes. Meanwhile, place the stock in a saucepan and bring to a gentle boil, add the rice and stir well. Cook for 12 minutes or until the rice is cooked but still firm to the bite. Add the pumpkin and tomatoes. Cook for 6 minutes or until most of the stock has been absorbed and the rice tender.

WT *Remember food is first eaten with the eye. Garnish risottos with bright and vibrant herbs or the zest of a lemon. The puckery citrus compliments the creaminess of the risotto beautifully while flecks of fresh herbs add freshness and fragrance.*

Rissoles

Makes 4

- *1 onion, peeled and diced*
- *1 clove garlic, crushed*
- *500g lean beef mince*
- *½ cup (50g) quick oats*

Preheat oven to 180°C. Sauté onion and garlic in a nonstick frying pan over medium / high heat in 1 tablespoon of water. Mix sautéed onion and garlic in a large bowl with the mince and oats and season with sea salt and cracked pepper. Form the mixture into meatballs and place on a baking tray. Bake for 25 minutes, turning after 15 minutes, or until cooked.

WT **NOTE:** *Those with a wheat allergy can eat uncontaminated oats (i.e., oats marked wheat-free), however those with a gluten intolerance or coeliacs cannot. Substitute oats with brown rice or grated gluten free breadcrumbs. For a yummy meatball dinner, make the exact mixture but roll into the size of golf balls. Cook in a large nonstick frying pan until browned all over. Add 1½ cups of the yummy homemade* **Napolitana Sauce***, page 56. Simmer gently together until hot and bubbly. Serve over rice.*

Steak with Onion Marmalade

Serves 4

- *2 rib fillet steaks, each 2cm thick*
- *2 tablespoons (40ml) olive oil*
- *2 onions, peeled and sliced*
- *2 tablespoons brown sugar*

Oil the steaks (this helps conduct the heat from the pan to the meat quickly) and season with sea salt and cracked pepper. Place the steaks into a hot nonstick frying pan and cook for 4 minutes, turn once and cook for another 4 minutes (for medium). Remove the steaks, cover with foil and rest. In the same pan, keeping the juices and oil, add the onions and cook for 5 minutes, or until just translucent. Reduce the heat, add the brown sugar and 2 tablespoons of water and cook for 10 minutes, stirring frequently, until sweetly caramelised. Serve the steaks dolloped with the onion marmalade and these wedges.

Sweet Potato & Rosemary Wedges

Serves 4

- *1 kg sweet potato*
- *1 tablespoon (20ml) olive oil*
- *¼ cup fresh rosemary leaves*
- *½ tablespoon lemon zest*

Preheat oven to 180°C. Wash and cut the sweet potato into wedges. Place into a bowl and toss with oil, spread onto a baking tray and sprinkle with rosemary. Bake for 30 minutes, or until golden. Sprinkle with lemon zest and season with sea salt to serve.

Sultana Stuffed Chicken

Serves 2

- *4 boneless, skinless chicken breasts*
- *4 slices allergy-free prosciutto*
- *⅓ cup sultana paste*
- *8 asparagus spears*

Preheat oven to 180°C. Carefully butterfly each chicken breast by cutting a slit down each breast and slicing almost through so it can be folded out. Lay a thin layer of prosciutto onto each. Spread with sultanas paste then asparagus spears, season with sea salt and cracked pepper. Roll up and lay seam side down in a baking tray, roast in the centre of the oven until chicken is cooked through, about 30 minutes. Remove from the oven to a serving platter. Let stand for 5 minutes, slice then serve.

Sultana Paste

- *1 cup sultanas*

In a blender, place the sultanas and blend to make a thick, sweet paste.

WT *Serve as an accompaniment with pork, chicken, sausages and ham. Dolloped atop curries, with fruit platters (way easier to make than quince paste) or enjoy for breakfast stirred through your favourite allergy-free cereals to naturally sweeten.*

Texan Pork Chops

Serves 4

- *4 pork chops (or cutlets)*
- *300g jar allergy-free salsa*
- *2 tablespoons jalapenos, chopped*

Season the chops or cutlets with sea salt and pepper. Heat a nonstick frying pan over medium / high, cook the cutlets for 3 to 4 minutes on each side, or until golden brown and cooked through. Remove cutlets from heat and rest for at least 2 minutes. Return pan to heat with pan juices, add the jalapenos and sauté for 30 seconds. Add the salsa, reduce the heat and simmer for 3 to 4 minutes allowing time for the flavours to develop. Serve the cutlets with the spicy salsa.

WT *To make your own **Homemade Salsa**: Heat 1 tablespoon (20ml) olive oil in a saucepan over medium heat. Add 1 onion finely chopped and cook, stirring, for 3 to 4 minutes or until soft. Add 1 finely chopped long red chilli and ½ chopped green capsicum. Cook for 2 minutes or until tender. Stir in 1 tablespoon tomato paste and 500g diced tomatoes. Bring mixture to the boil. Reduce heat and simmer, uncovered for 15 minutes or until thick. Remove from heat. Cool completely.*

Entertaining

Here are quick ideas when entertaining for guests with allergies.

- Cook some rice and turn into a beautiful rice salac with freshly chopped veggies, fresh herbs, and homemade citrus vinaigrette.

- Onto slices of fresh ham off the bone scatter grated carrot, finely chopped Spanish onion, chopped olives and fresh parsley. Season and roll, secure with a toothpick.

- Cut up potatoes, toss them in olive oil, fresh rosemary, salt and pepper and bake at 180°C for 40 minutes. Serve warm with the Quick Tomato Chutney on page 64.

- Grill pineapple slices with cracked pepper and honey.

- Be very mindful of cross contamination. Cleaning knives, chopping boards, pans and hands are simple ways to avoid this.

Apricot Chicken Balls

Makes 24

- *1 cup chopped sweet potato*
- *½ cup (60g) shredded coconut*
- *500g lean chicken mince*
- *12 dried apricots, finely chopped*

Preheat the oven to 180°C and line a baking tray with baking paper. In a small saucepan bring 2 cups (500ml) water to the boil. Add the sweet potato and boil for 4 minutes, or until tender. Drain, transfer to a large mixing bowl and mash well. Cool before adding chicken, apricots and coconut, season with sea salt and cracked pepper and mix until well combined. Roll into tablespoon sized balls and place on the prepared tray. Bake for around 20 to 22 minutes, turning half way, or until the chicken is cooked through and golden. Alternatively, fry in a little oil on the stovetop. These are sensational served with a dipping sauce made from mixing a little curry powder into Coyo.

WT *For a deliciously easy **Thai Chicken Meatballs**: Place 500g chicken mince in a large bowl, add half a red onion finely chopped, ¼ cup freshly chopped coriander, 1 teaspoon minced ginger and 1 large red chilli, seeds removed and finely chopped. Season with sea salt and cracked pepper, mix thoroughly then chill. Roll into balls and bake as above.*

BerryNiceSicles

Makes 6

- *250g strawberries, hulled, washed*
- *400ml can coconut milk, shaken*
- *150g blueberries*

Place the strawberries and ⅓ of the coconut milk in a blender and pulse until smooth. Pour evenly among 6 ice block moulds. Place in the freezer for 1 hour or until almost set. Remove ice blocks and divide half the remaining coconut milk evenly among moulds. Tap the moulds on a work surface to smooth tops. Place in the freezer for 1 hour or until almost set. Add blueberries and the remaining coconut milk into a blender and process until smooth. Remove moulds from the freezer. Pour blueberry mixture evenly among moulds. Insert wooden pop sticks into the centres. Return to the freezer for a further 2 hours or until set. Remove from moulds and serve immediately.

WT *Any extra can be frozen in ice cube trays for bite-size treats or added to smoothies. **NOTE:** I used full fat coconut milk as it is the fat content that helps prevent ice-cream from crystallising during freezing.*

Better Than Fries

Makes 24 wedges

- *4 large unpeeled potatoes, scrubbed*
- *3 tablespoons (60ml) olive oil*

Preheat the oven to 200°C. Prick each potato all over and rub with a little of the oil. Place them directly on the oven shelf and bake for 40 to 45 minutes, remove and cool enough to handle. Cut each potato in half lengthways and then into quarters. Scoop out the flesh, retaining for another use such as mash, and leaving a layer of potato at least 1cm thick on the skin. Arrange in a single layer, skin-side down on a baking tray and brush all over with the remaining oil. Bake for 15 to 20 minutes, turning half way through, until crisp and golden brown. Season with sea salt and cracked pepper to serve.

WT *Serve these with the yummy **Homemade Salsa** page 92. For flavour variations, bake the fries sprinkled with a mix of fresh or dried thyme or rosemary, or paprika and cinnamon.*

Choc-Banana Freezies

Makes 6

- *¼ cup (30g) shredded coconut*
- *50g dried mango, finely chopped*
- *3 large, ready to eat bananas*
- *150g allergy-free dark chocolate, broken*

Line a baking tray with wax paper. On two separate plates scatter coconut and mango. Peel bananas and cut in half. Stick each half on a paddle pop stick. Place the chocolate into a ceramic dish, melt on high in the microwave, stirring every 30 seconds until nice and smooth. Dip one banana into the melted chocolate, coating thoroughly. Sprinkle with coconut and set on prepared tray. Repeat the process, but sprinkle with mango. When finished, place the '*banana-pops*' in the freezer for 3 to 4 hours. Once frozen, wrap individually in cling wrap and return to freezer until ready to serve.

WT *You can experiment with toppings such as allergy-free sprinkles, crushed freeze-dried strawberries, finely chopped dried apples, dates or raw cacao powder.*

DeeeeLICIOUS Dates

OMG OMG OMG OMG *(that is all I have to say!!)*

Makes 16

- *16 Medjool dates*
- *8 slices allergy-free prosciutto, sliced in half lengthways*
- *1 tablespoon (20g) allergy-free wholegrain mustard*
- *2 tablespoons (60g) raw honey*

Preheat oven to 180°C. Using a small sharp knife, cut a slit in each date and remove stone. Mix the raw honey and mustard together in a small bowl, then spoon half a teaspoonful of the mixture into each date. Wrap a piece of prosciutto around each date, and arrange seam side down on a baking tray. Bake for 10 minutes or until the prosciutto is nice and crisp.

Homemade Lemonade

Serves 4

- *8 lemons, plus more for garnishing if desired*
- *1½ cups (330g) sugar*
- *7 cups of water*

Roll each lemon firmly on a hard surface, as this will make them easier to juice and increase the amount of juice extracted. Zest 2 to 3 lemons and set aside. In a pot over medium heat, add sugar, lemon zest and 2 cups of water. Simmer gently for 5 minutes, stirring until sugar has dissolved and the mixture has a light yellow colour. Do not boil. Remove from heat. Juice the lemons and pour the juice into a large pitcher. Add the sugar mixture and the remaining 5 cups of water and stir well. Refrigerate until ready to serve. Then fill glasses with ice and pour in the lemonade.

WT *Dress up your drinks with pretty ice cubes. A homemade lemonade looks especially pretty served with ice cubes that have been frozen with a mint leaf in them or a thin slice of lemon.*

Oven Roasted Crisps

Serves 6

- *2 potatoes, peeled*
- *300g sweet potato, peeled*
- *2 large beetroots, washed*
- *3 tablespoons (60ml) olive oil*

Preheat the oven 180°C. Line two baking trays with baking paper. For best results, use a mandolin (readily purchased from any homeware store) or alternatively a really sharp knife and a steady hand. Starting with the potatoes, hold the first at the top, then press down and glide across the blade (just keep your fingers nice and high!). Repeat with second potato, sweet potato and finally the beetroot. Add all to a large bowl and gently toss in the olive oil (careful not to over do it, too much oil won't result in crispy chips!). Sprinkle with sea salt. Lay each slice flat onto the baking trays. Bake for 10 to 15 minutes or until nice and crisp. Cool completely before serving with your favourite allergy-free dip.

Party Canapes

Makes 24

- *250g rockmelon*
- *1 mango*
- *½ cup sultanas*
- *1 tablespoon pomegranate seeds*

Peel the rockmelon and mango, and from the flesh cut as many heart shapes as you can. Place the shapes on a serving platter. In a blender, blend the sultanas to make a thick, sweet paste. Place a small amount of paste atop each piece of fruit and sprinkle with pomegranate seeds.

WT *Another really nice topping idea is to smash fresh raspberries and a little honey into coconut cream. Serve dolloped on top of fresh mango, with a slice of fresh raspberry.*

Raspberry Cupcakes

Makes 24

- *500g allergy-free vanilla cake mix*
- *375ml can creaming soda (any carbonated drink will work)*

Preheat oven to 180°C. Line two 12-cup cupcake tins with patty papers. In a large bowl, pour the cake mix, create a well and add the creaming soda. Using a wooden spoon stir the mixture until just combined. Spoon the mixture evenly across each cup and bake for 12 to 14 minutes.

Raspberry Icing

- *300g raspberries, fresh or frozen*
- *2½ tablespoons Nuttelex, softened*
- *2–3 cups (200–300g) allergy-free icing sugar*
- *½ teaspoon freshly squeezed lemon juice*

Cook the raspberries in a saucepan over medium heat, stirring frequently until they are broken down into a sauce. Pour the sauce through a fine mesh strainer to remove the seeds, and then pour the raspberry sauce back into the saucepan. Simmer until the sauce reduces to about ¼ of a cup. It will be a very rich and concentrated sauce. Set aside to cool. With a mixer, cream the Nuttelex on medium high speed for 2 minutes, until light and fluffy. Add 2 cups icing sugar, the cooled raspberry sauce and lemon juice. Continue mixing until smooth. Add more icing sugar if needed.

WT *Another delicious **Raspberry Icing** is to mix together 3 tablespoons of softened Nuttelex, 2 cups allergy-free icing sugar and 1 generous tablespoon of allergy-free raspberry jam … Simple!*

S'More Meatballs

Serves 12

- *½ cup semi-dried tomatoes, finely chopped*
- *1 onion, peeled and finely diced*
- *600g lean beef mince*
- *1 teaspoon oregano*

Preheat oven to 180°C. Place the ingredients in a large bowl (reserving the oil from the semi-dried tomatoes). Season with sea salt and cracked pepper and mix well. Form into balls. Add reserved oil to a nonstick frying pan and sauté for 6 minutes turning regularly or until cooked through.

WT *My kids love these with homemade **Napolitana Sauce** page 56. Simply brown the meatballs in a non-stick frying pan and pour over the sauce. Reduce the heat and simmer for 10 minutes. If you are adding other ingredients like store-bought pasta sauce or garlic powder make sure you review all food ingredient labels carefully to uncover potential allergens. I found my garlic powder contained soy – it pays to be a 'Label Detective'!*

Tapas Plate

Eggplant Tapenade

Serves 4

- *250g eggplant*
- *2 teaspoons (10ml) garlic infused olive oil*
- *½ lemon, juiced*
- *1 tablespoon chopped parsley*

Grill the eggplant turning occasionally, until the skins are charred. Cut them open and scoop out the flesh. Place all the ingredients into a food processor or blender and season with sea salt and cracked pepper and blend briefly. Alternatively, mash the eggplant flesh and beat in the rest of the ingredients. Serve at room temperature with your favourite dipping sticks.

White Bean Dip

Serves 4

- *420g can cannellini beans, drained and rinsed*
- *1 garlic clove, crushed*
- *2 tablespoons (40ml) fresh lemon juice*
- *⅓ cup (80ml) olive oil*

Place all ingredients in a blender. Season with sea salt and cracked pepper and blend until nice and smooth. Transfer the puree to a small bowl. Serve with freshly sliced veggie sticks, roasted veggie sticks or allergy-free crackers.

WT *This simple yet delicious dip can be used as a base to create lots of flavoured dips. Try adding sun dried tomato, marinated artichoke hearts and fresh herbs to name a few. This easy dip is also delicious served with grilled lamb, chicken or beef.*

Sweet Things

Chocolate (OMG!) Brownie

Makes 16 slices

- *2 cups (350g) allergy-free self raising flour*
- *2 cups (400g) caster sugar*
- *¾ cup (70g) raw cacao powder*
- *1 cup (250ml) vegetable oil*

Preheat oven to 180°C. Line a 20 x 30cm baking tray with baking paper. In a large bowl, stir together the flour, sugar, cacao powder, and ½ teaspoon of sea salt. Add the vegetable oil and 1 cup (250ml) water and mix until blended. Spread evenly in the tray. Bake for 30 minutes or until the top is no longer shiny. Cool before cutting into squares.

WT *If entertaining, dust lightly with allergy-free icing sugar before slicing for an elegant black and white contrast and top with fresh seasonal berries.*

Coconut Cake with Strawberry Jam

Serves 8

- *1 cup (120g) desiccated coconut*
- *1 cup (250ml) coconut milk*
- *½ cup (100g) caster sugar*
- *1 cup (175g) allergy-free self raising flour*

Preheat oven 180°C. Place all ingredients in a bowl and mix. Line a loaf tin with baking paper and pour the mixture in. Bake for 40 minutes or until a skewer inserted comes out clean.

Microwave Strawberry Jam

Makes 1½ cups

- *250g strawberries, hulled, chopped*
- *½ lemon, juiced*
- *½ cup (100g) caster sugar*

Place all the ingredients into a large microwave-safe heatproof bowl. Microwave, uncovered, for 12 to 15 minutes on high, stirring every 3 minutes until thick and *'jam-like'. NOTE: The jam should still be a little runny as it will thicken on cooling.*

Date & Apple Spring Rolls

Serves 4

- *100g dried apple, chopped*
- *12 dried dates, pitted and chopped*
- *8 allergy-free spring roll wrappers*
- *½ cup (125ml) vegetable oil*

Soak chopped apple and dates in boiling water until tender. Drain off liquid and refrigerate to cool. Place a generous tablespoon full of date and apple mixture on a spring roll wrapper and roll, fold in the sides and fold again. Heat the oil in a frying pan and shallow fry the rolls until nice and golden, turning throughout. Dust with allergy-free icing sugar to serve (optional, but pretty!).

WT *These are just delicious, you can alter the flavour by alternating the fillings. My kids love banana and cinnamon, mango and coconut drizzled with pure maple syrup and a mixture of chopped banana and mango sprinkled with brown sugar … yummy!*

Ice Cream Palate

Chocolate Ice Cream

Serves 4

- *3 bananas, sliced into coins and frozen*
- *4 tablespoons raw cacao powder*
- *1 teaspoon (5ml) vanilla extract*

Line a loaf tin with baking paper. Blend the frozen bananas in a food processor until they are the consistency of soft-serve ice cream. Add the cacao and vanilla and blend for 10 seconds, or until well combined. Serve immediately or freeze the mixture until ready to serve.

Strawberry Ice Cream

Serves 2

- *1 banana, peeled, sliced into coins and frozen*
- *1 handful of strawberries, frozen*
- *2 tablespoons (40ml) coconut cream*
- *1 teaspoon (5ml) pure vanilla extract*

Place all the ingredients into a blender or food processor. Blend together just enough to achieve a really thick lovely consistency. This ice cream is best eaten immediately.

WT *For a delicious, nutritious **Mango Sorbet** see 4 Ingredients Diabetes page 44 – it's just divine!*

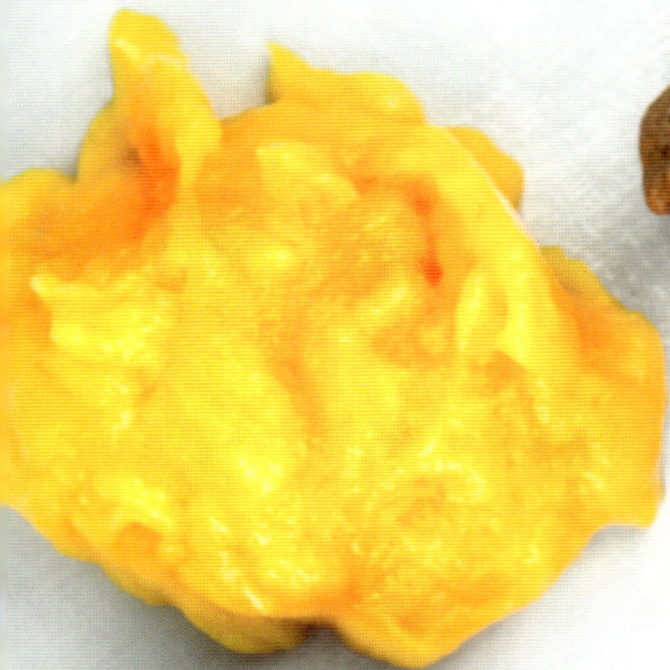

Pineapple Flowers

Makes 12

- *Olive oil spray*
- *1 small pineapple, peeled*
- *½ cup (125ml) coconut cream, whipped*
- *12 red grapes, sliced crosswise 80% through*

Preheat oven to 125°C. Gently spray a muffin tray with olive oil. Using a sharp knife, slice the pineapple crosswise into very thin slices. Lay each slice across the cup of the tray and gently push down, forming a bowl. Bake until the tops look dried, about 40 minutes. Cool, then transfer to a serving plate. Spoon a teaspoon of whipped coconut cream into each and stud with a red grape. Serve immediately.

Whipped Coconut Cream

Makes 1 cup

- *400g can coconut milk, refrigerated overnight*
- *2 tablespoons allergy-free icing sugar*
- *½ teaspoon pure vanilla extract*

Open the can of coconut milk and scoop the top layer of the creamy white, goodness into a decent sized mixing bowl (drink or freeze the coconut water for smoothies). Blend the chunks of coconut milk with a hand mixer on high speed for 15 seconds, just until the mixture turns to liquid. Sift in the icing sugar and mix until combined. Add the vanilla extract and blend on high speed for 1 minute, or until light and creamy.

Poached Bananas in Coconut Cream

Serves 4

- *100g palm sugar*
- *1½ cups (375ml) water*
- *3 bananas, peeled and cut into thirds*
- *½ cup (125ml) coconut cream*

Mix the sugar and water in a frying pan over medium heat and bring to the boil. Reduce heat and cook until the liquid forms a sweet, sticky syrup that coats the back of a spoon. Add the bananas and gently cook, turning regularly until they are warmed through. Place the bananas and syrup in a serving dish. In a separate saucepan mix the coconut cream and ¼ teaspoon sea salt and heat gently for 3 to 4 minutes. Do not boil. Drizzle the coconut cream over the bananas and serve.

WT *Often you have herbs and spices from previous recipes – this was the case when I made this dish. I added star anise to the coconut cream and sprinkled with a little fresh mint to serve … Totally yum!* ☺

Raspberry & Lime Sorbet

Serves 8

- *1 cup (200g) caster sugar*
- *500g raspberries (fresh or frozen, thawed)*
- *1 lime, juice and zest*

Line a loaf tin with baking or wax paper. Add 1 cup (250ml) of water to the sugar in a saucepan and bring to a gentle boil, stirring constantly to dissolve the sugar. Lower the heat and simmer for 3 minutes. Remove from heat and completely chill. In a blender, purée raspberries. Mix the purée with the syrup, add ¾ cup (185ml) water, the lime juice and zest. Pour into the prepared tin and freeze for at least 4 hours.

WT *Another variation is my super easy* **Pina Colada Soft-Serve***: Cut enough for 2 cups of fresh pineapple and freeze overnight. When ready to serve, place the pineapple in a food processor, add ¼ cup (60ml) coconut cream and a splash of raw honey. Blend until nice and smooth and serve immediately sprinkled with a little lime zest.*

Toffee Web

Toffee is a way to decorate and enhance simple, fresh produce. It is basically sugar and a little water but add heat … and the magic really begins!

Makes 4 Webs

- *1 cup (200g) sugar*
- *⅓ (80ml) cup water*

From a sheet of wax paper, cut four 10 x 10cm square pieces. In a saucepan stir the water and sugar over low heat until the sugar dissolves. Then, increase the heat and bring the sugar to the boil. Brush the sides of the pot with a wet pastry brush to dissolve any remaining sugar crystals. Watch for the toffee to change colour and remove from heat when it begins to turn light golden, it will continue to cook after it has been removed, so don't leave it too long as it will harden before you can use it. Using the tines of a fork, and working quickly, dip into the toffee and spread over the square of wax paper, working the toffee back and forth creating a 'web-like' feature. Repeat with remaining three sheets. Return to the first sheet and gently mould the toffee into a semi-circular web. Place on a tray, repeat then refrigerate to harden. Fill with all sorts of delicious, fresh seasonal fruit. Serve with a dollop of **Whipped Coconut Cream**, page 128.

WT *Use caution with toffee as it is very hot and can cause severe burns.*

Tropical Rice Pudding

Serves 4

- *1 cup (185g) short-grain brown rice*
- *400ml coconut milk*
- *2 tablespoons grated palm sugar (I used two cubes)*
- *1 ripe pineapple, halved*

Combine rice and 2 cups (500ml) of water in a medium saucepan over high heat. Bring to a boil, reduce to a simmer and cook until water has been absorbed and rice is tender, 20 to 25 minutes. Meanwhile, cut the pineapple in half including its crown. Scoop out 90% of its filling, discard the hard core and finely chop the remaining. Into the rice, stir the coconut milk, palm sugar and pineapple; stir, simmering, for 6 minutes. Serve the delicious pudding scooped into the pineapple halves for all to enjoy.

Thank You

One man can be a crucial
ingredient on a team,
but he cannot make a team!

Kareem Abdul-Jabbor

Reach Out
Join our Foodie Family

At 4 Ingredients we cultivate a family of busy people all bound together by the desire to create good, healthy, homemade meals quickly, easily and economically.

Our aim is to save us all precious time and money in the kitchen. If this is you too, then we invite you to join our growing family where we share kitchen wisdom daily.

If you have a favourite recipe, or a tip that has worked for you in your kitchen and think others would enjoy it, please join our family at:

facebook.com/4ingredientspage

@4ingredients

4 Ingredients Channel

4ingredients.com.au

@4ingredients

With Love
Kim

Index

Bibliography

Websites

www.Coyo.com.au/index.htm

www.livestrong.com/article/351598-is-eating-fruit-for-breakfast-healthy/#ixzz2Ur1TfHEQ

What is an allergy?
What is anaphylaxsis?
Who is at risk?
www.allergyfacts.org.au

About Us
A-Z Allergies
www.allergy.org.nz

ASCIA Allergy and Immune Diseases in Australia (AIDA) Report
www.allergy.org.au

The allergy-friendly cook
www.cybelepascal.com

Books & Magazines

Prescott, Dr. Susan. L. **The Allergy Epidemic: A Mystery of Modern Life**. UWA Publishing, Crawley Western Australia, 6009.

Pascal, Cybele. **The Whole Foods Allergy Cookbook: Two Hundred Gourmet & Homestyle Recipes for the Food Allergic Family**. Vital Health Pulbishing PO BOX 152, Ridgefield, CT 06877.